Old CARNOUSTIE

by
Fiona Scharlau

The Carnoustie Young Men's Christian Association football team of 1919–1920.

© Angus Council Cultural Services 2002
First published in the United Kingdom, 2002,
by Stenlake Publishing
Telephone / Fax: 01290 551122

ISBN 1 84033 195 X

ACKNOWLEDGEMENTS

The author would like to thank the staff of Cultural Services and the Angus Local Studies Centre for their help and moral support. Thanks are also gratefully extended to Alasdair Sutherland of Carnoustie Library and Donald McMahon for their assistance.

FURTHER READING

The books listed below were used by the author during her research. None of them are available from Stenlake Publishing. Those interested in finding out more are advised to contact their local bookshop or reference library.

Statistical Account of Scotland
New Statistical Account of Scotland
Annie L. Thompson, *Carnoustie In Old Postcards*, 1998
James Baillie, *The Old Parish Church of Carnoustie: The First Hundred Years 1837–1937*, 1937
Carnoustie Local History Group, *Carnoustie Through the Ages*, 1997
James Fotheringham, *Carnoustie Sketches*, 1889
Donald McDougall, *The Carnoustie Story*, n.d.
Carnoustie Golf Course Committee, *Carnoustie and its Golf Courses*, n.d.
Fiona Scharlau, *Carnoustie: Brighton of the North*,
     www.angus.gov.uk/history/features
Angus Local Studies Centre research files
Carnoustie scrapbooks 1914–1952

The staff of McKay & Stewart's plumbing business (and one of their children) stand outside the shop at 100 High Street to be photographed in 1913.

INTRODUCTION

Of the seven Angus burghs, Carnoustie is the youngest. It only became a settlement of any size in the nineteenth century and a burgh in 1895. The name is undoubtedly Celtic, although does not appear in written form until 1539 when the farm of 'Carnusie' is mentioned. While the first part of the name is certainly from the Gaelic for 'hill', the latter half is more obscure with one possible meaning being 'firwood'.

Carnoustie formed part of the lands of the church of Barry which were granted to Balmerino Abbey in 1229. The barony (as such a collection of lands and the title that went with it was known) was gifted to Sir Philip de Valoniis, Lord High Chamberlain, about 1172. In 1224 his granddaughter Christina married Sir Peter Maule and the barony passed to the Maule family. The title later passed to the Panmure family, and 600 years later is still held by one of their descendants, the Earl of Dalhousie. Those parts of the Panmure estate which had not already been disposed of were broken up and sold in 2001.

In 1792 the Carnoustie estate was purchased from the Panmure family by a former employee, Major Philip. He had made a fortune in India and returned to Angus to enjoy a comfortable retirement. Philip granted the first feu in 1797 to one Thomas Lowson, and seeing the commercial potential of feuing offered inducements to other settlers. A village began to grow and was at first contained within Barry parish, later spilling over the Lochty Burn into Panbride parish.

With the march of industrialisation and its proximity to Dundee (which was subsequently connected to the village by rail), Carnoustie steadily grew into a town. It became home to a wide variety of industrial concerns including the Winter family's boot and shoemaking factory, golf club makers such as Simpson's, the Panmure jute works, the vitriol works and more recently D. J. Laing construction and MacKays jam factory. Employers such as these attracted growing numbers of people seeking work, and by the early twentieth century the population had increased to approximately 4,500. The presence of the railway was a magnet to middle class families who settled in the town from where their male breadwinners commuted to work in Dundee.

In the late nineteenth century a town council was established in Carnoustie, implementing various improvements including the installation of kerbs by the roadside, the laying down of concrete paths, the introduction of street lighting and the securing of an improved water supply.

Carnoustie became very popular as a holiday resort on account of its beneficial fresh sea air, and promoted itself as the Brighton of the North. As a resort, its heyday lasted from the late nineteenth century to the outbreak of World War II. The railway brought holidaymakers and day trippers from all over Scotland, and the town's attractions were promoted vigorously by the council. These included the pierrots and three excellent golf courses (the most popular attraction for male visitors). Carnoustie has staged six golf Open championships, the most recent one taking place in 1999.

Modern Carnoustie is a very popular residential town, retaining a variety of industry. While the attractions of its beach have been eroded by package holidays to warmer destinations, the popularity and reputation of its golf courses continues to grow.

The medieval church at Barry may originally have been dedicated to St Marnoch, and then to St Stephen. It was rebuilt in 1800 and stood in the centre of the old village of Barry until its demolition in 1965.

Carnoustie is largely situated in the parish of Barry, bounded by the Lochty Burn, beyond which lies the neighbouring parish of Panbride. Until the young town constructed its own place of worship in 1837 its inhabitants had to make the long walk to Barry parish church, illustrated here, to attend church. Thomas Lowson, considered to be the founder of the town, was buried in its churchyard in 1856. In 1797, the year that Lowson settled in the area, parishioners disaffected by the threat of war from Napoleon rioted at Barry manse. Another famous Carnoustian, Sir John Kirk, a companion of David Livingstone on his second Zambezi expedition, was baptised in the old church.

The present mill at Barry was built in 1814 on the site of a much older mill which had been destroyed by fire. It operated as a working mill until the early 1980s when the mill lade collapsed. Despite being in a state of decay, the National Trust for Scotland took it over and repaired it. Since 1992 it has been open to visitors as a working meal mill.

PANBRIDE CHURCH, CARNOUSTIE.

2611.

Carnoustie straddles the parishes of Panbride and Barry. Panbride Church is built on the thirteenth century site of an older building dedicated to St Brigid. It was the church used by the Maule family, and many family members are buried within its walls. William Ramsay-Maule had the present building constructed in 1851. An interesting feature is the ancient set of jougs bolted to the wall beside the entrance. These would have been used to punish a variety of minor transgressions committed by the parishioners.

Carnoustie bay sweeps in a wide gentle curve but its grace belies its danger. It is hazardous to shipping and many vessels have foundered within sight of safety during severe storms. In 1913 the Dutch ship *Aefina* sank in Carnoustie bay with the loss of everyone except her captain, Mr de Yonge. After a night spent clinging to the wreckage of his vessel, de Yonge was rescued by Alexander Lamond, a local scout leader. Some time later Captain de Yonge wrote to the 'Mayor' of Carnoustie concerning the wreck of the *Aefina*. Having been involved in a second wreck in which he had lost all his mementoes of the *Aefina*, he wrote requesting some souvenirs of his old ship. By a strange coincidence, during World War II, Alexander Lamond was held as a prisoner of war in Holland near to where de Yonge's family lived. They kept him supplied with parcels of food and clothing throughout the war.

The wide sweep of Carnoustie bay makes it a tempting place for children to paddle. Many postcards show Edwardian girls, and a few ladies, tucking up their skirts and enjoying a dip in the cool sea. The beach and seaside were Carnoustie's main attractions and the town promoted its healthy climate and invigorating sea bathing. Between 1904 and 1914 there was only one reported case of smallpox and eight of typhoid in the town, while infant mortality was also low. Carnoustie was described as the Home of Health and Happiness, and the Brighton of the North.

Castle Building, Carnoustie.   728

Carnoustie beach has always provided opportunities for the simple pleasures of playing in the sand and paddling. In 1924 the *Daily Mail* sponsored a sand-building competition, and in later years other sand-based games were introduced for children. One such was the tide game. Each child had to build a sand barrier against the incoming tide and the last barrier standing was the winner. There were many activities to enjoy in and around Carnoustie, and if a family got tired of the beach they could also play on the swings, enjoy a round of golf, have a game of bowls or tennis, watch the pierrots, enjoy a movie, take a charabanc ride into the country, go fishing at West Haven or enjoy a cup of tea at De Marco's.

8

Carnoustie was such a popular pre-1939 destination that extra trains were laid on at the weekends in the summer to cope with the large numbers travelling. The tunnel at the foot of Park Avenue became a busy access route to the beach. In the 1920s the *Carnoustie Guide and Gazette* often reported that the beach looked black as it was covered with so many people enjoying a stroll, sitting in the sun, playing on the giant slide or waiting their turn for a bathing coach. This picture gives a good indication of the size of the aptly named giant slide, erected in 1929. At the time many of the children complained that the adults were using it too much!

THE PADDLING POOL, CARNOUSTIE.

Other crowd-pleasers were added to the resort's range of attractions during the 1930s including the large paddling pool fed by the Lochty Burn and its shelter. The pool cost £92 to build and provided endless hours of fun for children. Paddling pool sports were very popular, while if it rained games would be held in the Beach Hall (opened in 1934). A favourite pool game was the scramble. Ten shillings worth of half pennies were thrown into the pool, which instantly became a seething mass of bodies.

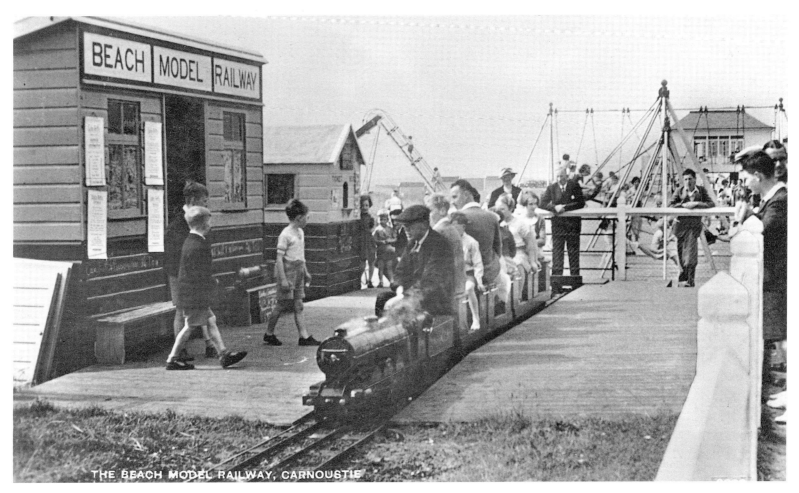

THE BEACH MODEL RAILWAY, CARNOUSTIE

The model railway on Carnoustie's beach operated for only two years, ceasing with the outbreak of World War II in 1939. It was opened on 12 May 1937, the Coronation day of King George VI and Queen Elizabeth. Harry Ferguson constructed the miniature railway but the idea had originated with his neighbour, Bailie Fred Murray, a steam enthusiast. Ferguson was offered the site for a peppercorn rent and although he bought the engine built the carriages himself. The railway ran for 140 yards between the swings and the paddling pool and travelled alongside the main railway line. It had a proper station, where tickets were bought, and an engine shed. Not surprisingly it was a firm favourite with children. Many Sunday schools chose Carnoustie and its miniature railway as the venue for their summer excursion, sometimes travelling to the town from as far away as Glasgow.

The pierrots' al fresco concerts were one of Carnoustie's biggest attractions. Pierrots – buffoon figures that wore long-sleeved white robes – were an essential part of every Edwardian seaside resort. They stemmed from the tradition of the commedia dell'arte and superseded minstrels who had been the fashion previously (minstrels were white performers who 'blacked up' using make-up). Entrepreneurs recognised an opportunity to make money and hired performing pitches from local councils. This was quite lucrative for the local authorities who in return ensured that the lucky troupe would not face any competition. The pierrots performed songs, dances and comedy sketches on wooden stages erected on the links. Some troupes were truly dreadful, while others were very good, but Carnoustie always attracted quality acts that viewed the resort as a step on the way to fame.

CHORUS-
She sifted thistles,
Twisted thick thistles,
Sifting the twisted thick
thistles sat she.
And with strong string
strung them in sheaves sheepishly
For thistles she sifted,
thick twisted thistles,
And Cissy, her sister,
assisted in sifting
the thick thistles
her sister sifted.

Gilbert Payne and the White Coons (a name that would not be acceptable in modern times) entertained Carnoustie's holidaymakers from 1900 to 1914. With his slogan 'There is no pleasure without Payne', Gilbert Payne was very well known in the world of the music hall. In his day he was rated as one of the six best comedians in the country, and in the same league as his contemporary Harry Lauder. His trademark character was Mr Bungle who sported a big red wig. Payne was the White Coons' comic but also managed the shows, engaged the entertainers and staged the numbers. His troupe performed two shows daily after a morning rehearsal. It was a hard life, as he organised similar shows in Broughty Ferry, Arbroath and St Andrews too. Payne was the first to propose that instead of a temporary wooden stage for the pierrots a concert hall should be built. In 1914 he offered to provide such a hall at a cost of £250 and lease it to the council for five years, after which they would have the option of buying it. Nothing happened. Payne didn't apply for the pierrot concession at Carnoustie the following year, instead pursuing his career as a variety star. He returned to the town in 1934 with the Jolly Jesters, the same year in which the council opened the Beach Hall. His slogan then was 'Not al fresco, not revue. But something novel! Something new!'

13

In 1915 Birmingham-based Leo Bliss and the Busy Bees came to Carnoustie, becoming regular performers in the town (this view of them dates from 1925). Mr Bliss's advertising slogan was a clever play on names: 'After 14 years of Payne, you need a little Bliss'. His real name was Leo Petro Ameghino and he was a vaudeville artist with a reputation as a safe comedian who could 'make a mummy laugh'. He worked with his wife Dorothy B. Lloyd, another talented comedian, and between them they introduced a number of new features to the pierrot shows. These included local Carnoustie artists, singing and novelty competitions for the audience, and special request evening shows. If it rained Bliss arranged for the concerts to be relocated to the YMCA hall. He also introduced a series of end of season benefit concerts for each member of the troupe. The songs used by the Busy Bees were described as 'absolute winners' and came from successful and well-known songwriters; in fact the troupe had the reputation of being the best on the Scottish east coast. Bliss also ran another troupe which operated in resorts including Dunoon. After Leo Bliss died the act was taken over by his widow.

On 30 June 1934 Provost Ramsay opened the Links Hall, a facility that had been proposed twenty years earlier by Gilbert Payne of the White Coons. It was built in the Art Deco style and was designed for a variety of entertainments from pierrot shows to concerts, theatricals and dances. At the time of its opening it was described as the last word in comfort. Gilbert Payne's Jolly Jesters were the first to perform there for the 1934 season. The hall brought a new degree of comfort to its audience but much of the charm of the al fresco shows was lost.

The children in the foreground are digging in the sand, paying no attention to the seaside mission service being held behind them in the shelter of the Links Pavilion. The pavilion was later extended to incorporate a bathing station and tearoom.

Carnoustie had attractions other than the beach and its associated pleasures. From the 1930s onwards visitors didn't have to walk to the High Street to enjoy afternoon tea. The Links Pavilion stood adjacent to the new concert hall and the tennis courts and after its extension incorporated a tearoom. Post-World War II holiday activities focused on this area. The town council, in conjunction with the entertainment manager Bill Cumming, organised a variety of competitions such as Cute Kiddies and Holiday Princesses. Since this photograph was taken the putting green in the foreground has been turned into a rest garden.

A charming Edwardian view of families gathered to listen to the Sunday afternoon concert at the Links bandstand. This was situated close to the Dalhousie Golf Club, where the modern car park now stands. It was built in 1864 and regularly featured Sunday afternoon concerts by the burgh band, which played both religious and military music. Visiting military bands also contributed to the programme. In 1924 an evening concert was introduced which featured a programme of dance music. Strictly speaking dancing was not permitted on the Links under a burgh by-law, so this was quite a daring move. The bandstand was demolished during the 1960s.

THE ROCK GARDENS, CARNOUSTIE

2616

The Bruce Hotel was built in 1892 and was the most fashionable hotel in Carnoustie. It drew its clients not only from Britain but exotic overseas locations such as New York, Java, Shanghai and Hong Kong, and was named after its owner Mary Bruce. She once complained to the town council that the pierrots on the links were too noisy in the evenings and that they kept her guests' children awake. The hotel originally had 74 bedrooms, with a new wing of about 30 rooms added in the 1930s to cope with demand. In April 1921 the cast of *Christie Johnston*, a movie filmed in Auchmithie, stayed at the hotel. Other famous guests have included Charlie Chaplin, Margaret Thatcher and Yehudi Menuin. The hotel has now been converted into apartments.

A view of the links showing the tennis courts, the Bruce Hotel and the golf courses in the distance. The wide open space of the links made it possible for an unusual attraction to be offered in 1931 when pleasure flights from Carnoustie were introduced. The small aircraft landed between the bandstand and Barry Burn bridge. Today the Carnoustie Golf Course Hotel stands on the site of the old starter's box, and the tennis court in the foreground has been replaced by the leisure centre's car park.

The tennis courts were built and operated by Carnoustie Town Council and provided both an attraction to visitors and a source of income, generating £344 in 1920. The Links Pavilion is now the home of the rugby club and has been recently refurbished after a fire in 2001. Beach huts are no longer a part of the seaside view at Carnoustie. In recent years this part of the bay has undergone a great deal of protective work to limit coastal erosion.

The Setting Sun, Carnoustie, 731

This view from the links shows Links Parade and the clubhouse of Dalhousie Golf Club in the background. It was in Glencoe House on Links Parade that the famous composer Scott Skinner resided for some time during and after the First World War. In 1921 the *Guide and Gazette* launched a campaign to persuade the government to award Skinner a civil pension. They recalled that 'his short, sturdy figure in kilt and sporran, was once well-known on our streets while his stick waved out a merry salutation to rich and poor, male and female'. Skinner was involved in local concerts, including one remembered as outstanding at the Panmure Institute Hall in 1915. He also had many pupils throughout Angus, and would often dash off an air on the nearest available piece of paper before posting it to one of his pupils.

This 1911 view of Carnoustie provides an interesting view of the back gardens of the cottages in the vicinity of Links Parade. A water butt is visible over the roof in the foreground, collecting water for the household. Beyond, the roofline of the Bruce Hotel is just visible. Various factory chimneys including Winter's boot and shoe factory can also be glimpsed. The large grassy area to the left of the railway has now been built on.

Carnoustie benefited enormously from the opening of the Arbroath to Dundee railway in 1838. The trains brought increasing numbers of visitors and allowed businessmen to live in the town and commute to work in Dundee. In 1840 the Railway Hotel, now the Station Hotel, was built alongside the railway station to accommodate travellers. The Victorian station buildings have now been removed, although the footbridge next to the level crossing remains.

Burn and 18th Green, Old Course, Carnoustie

Carnoustie has a long and rich golfing heritage, and is considered to have one of the best courses in the world. Golf has been played on the town's links for as long as it has at St Andrews. The course has evolved over the years and three of golf's greats had a large influence on its design. Allan Robertson, often regarded as the game's first star, laid out a 10-hole course in the 1850s, and Tom Morris senior extended this to 18 holes around twenty years later. In 1926 James Braid, a five-times Open champion, modernised the course so successfully that the Open was held there five years later. The last substantial alterations were carried out between 1931 and 1937 by James Wright, chairman of Carnoustie Golf Course Committee. His legacy is a flexible, quality course to which the Open championship has returned regularly, most recently in 1999.

Putting Green the Links Carnoustie.

M. 379.

Golf was a popular pastime with ladies as well as men. At one time ladies had their own golf course, and although they still have two clubs of their own in the town – the Carnoustie Ladies and the Lochty Ladies – men and women now play the same course. The tenth hole of the Medal Course is named South America, apparently after Davie Nicoll, a young Aberdonian who planned to set off for South America in the early nineteenth century. He had enjoyed a farewell party the evening before his departure and at nightfall got as far as the future site of the tenth hole. He fell asleep there and the next day resolved to go no further, calling his new home South America to honour his old ambition!

This aerial view of Carnoustie shows many features of the town that have now disappeared. The High Street divides the picture, with a residential area comprised of fine Edwardian villas and large Victorian houses to its left. On the other side of the street the view is more industrial. At the top right is the railway goods yard where the present-day supermarket and its car park now stand. This area was also the site of a preserving factory that supplied tinned vegetables to the royal and merchant navies. (Carnoustie was once famous for its carrots but after a severe storm stripped away the topsoil carrot production never regained its former pre-eminence.) Gas was first introduced to the burgh in 1856 and later the town council built gasometers between Bonella Street and Fox Street. Below these the Pavilion cinema can be seen on Park Avenue. This was built in 1912 in the Art Nouveau style and stood until the 1970s, showing its first talkie, *Sunny Side Up*, in 1931. The large range of sheds between Park Avenue and Ferrier Street belonged to Winter's boot and shoe factory, which was established in the town by John Winter in 1851 and continued by his son Provost George Winter. The factory closed in 1952 with the loss of 130 jobs. All of its buildings have since been demolished.

The caption on the reverse of this photograph describes it as showing workers at the Carnoustie foundry. It was taken in the High Street, perhaps outside the shop of the photographer and tobacconist James Jolly, probably in the early days of World War I. The men are wearing an unusual variety of hats. Carnoustie's east end was where the town's industrial premises were located. These included the Taymouth engineering works, the vitriol works, Scroggie's boot and shoe factory and the Panmure works. In its heyday Carnoustie produced a vast range of products ranging from the Dalhousie car, golf clubs and chemicals to some of the world's largest diamond saws.

Carnoustie's High Street has changed very little since this 1905 postcard was sent. Only the buildings on the left have gone, with the library now occupying this spot but positioned further back from the road. The awning over the shop on the right advertises these premises as being home to 'The Leading House Agent' in town. When visitors arrived many of them would seek out a house agent to locate appropriate accommodation. It was traditional for large numbers of Carnoustie people to rent out part of their house or flat to visitors during the season. Visitors might occupy the best parlour and have the food they provided cooked by their landlady. In other cases families moved out entirely to stay with relatives in the country during the visitor season. The most affluent holidaymakers booked accommodation for a month. The mother and children would stay throughout this period while the father would spend a week with them and then return at weekends.

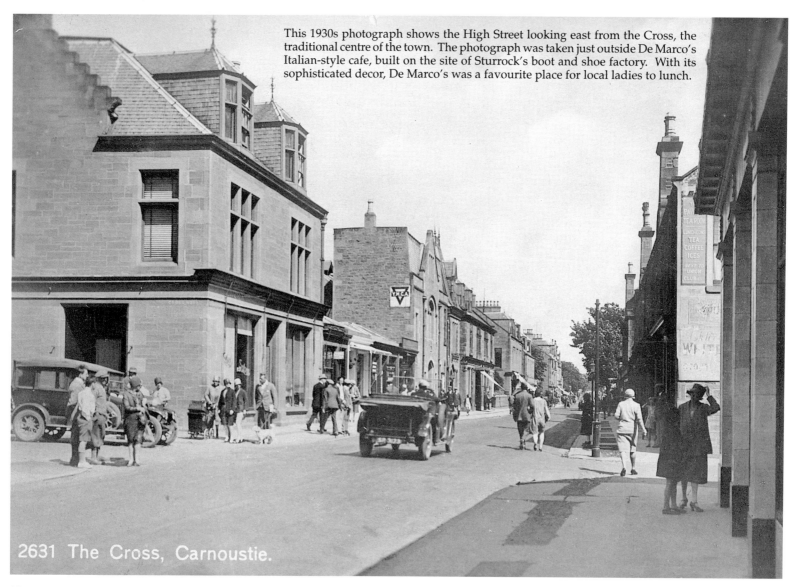

This 1930s photograph shows the High Street looking east from the Cross, the traditional centre of the town. The photograph was taken just outside De Marco's Italian-style cafe, built on the site of Sturrock's boot and shoe factory. With its sophisticated decor, De Marco's was a favourite place for local ladies to lunch.

2631 The Cross, Carnoustie.

The High Street looking east showing the Young Men's Christian Association building on the left. From 1875 when it arrived in the town, the YMCA was located in Bonella Street. To raise funds to build a hall and small meeting rooms, a bazaar was held in Dundee in 1881 and eight years later an impressive new building was erected in the High Street. At the time of its opening in 1889 the YMCA had insufficient funds to complete the exterior work and a temporary wood and plaster front was built (this photograph shows the completed frontage). The YMCA hall was a popular venue for indoor entertainments of all kinds, despite having a stage that prompted many complaints as it had been so badly constructed that it could not handle sets. Despite these difficulties, the hall was a blessing to the pierrots in 1922 when it turned out to be an exceptionally wet season. During the 1930s the YMCA was home to a debating club, billiards room and a roller rink.

An Edwardian view of the High Street looking east. The men in uniform are walking past a low cottage that was subsequently demolished and replaced by the Art Deco frontage of a garage; the building immediately behind them is now the Kinloch Hotel. This is one of the oldest buildings remaining on the High Street, and in 1893 was the first in Carnoustie to be lit by electricity. Awnings such as the ones visible here protecting the shop windows from the sunshine were a common sight until the 1960s.

High Street, Carnoustie

Dundee Street is a continuation of the High Street running westwards towards Barry Road. This elegant block of flats with their wrought iron balconies and shops below faces the site of the old St Stephen's Church, now demolished. The premises on the left is home to a typical Edwardian hardware shop, displaying many of its wares in the street and around the windows in order to entice customers inside.

Dundee Street, Carnoustie

4550

Carnoustie is situated on the fringe of some of the best agricultural land in Scotland. The large house on the hill in this picture is Morven House, which overlooks what was farmland until the turn of the twentieth century. A man is harvesting a field of wheat while an Edwardian lady and two boys stroll through the field that Wallace Street and Rose Street now stand on.

Lovers' Loan was once on the very edge of Carnoustie, its path following the walls around the grounds of Carnoustie House. This had been built by Major Philip, a former servant of the Earls of Panmure who made a fortune in India and returned to Carnoustie to spend his wealth. He feued out parcels of his land to tenants and Carnoustie grew as a result. The only surviving part of the house is the stable block, now the local authority recycling centre. The triangular area of land in the centre of this picture, between the two roads, was donated to the town council by the Lingard-Guthrie family of Carnoustie House, and additional trees were planted there in 1937 to celebrate the Coronation of King George VI. Although the road to the right was known informally as Lovers' Loan, its official name was West Path; this was mirrored by East Path (now Queen Street) on the other side of Carnoustie House's grounds. At the foot of West Path on the right is a smart row of terraced cottages built by shoe manufacturer John Winter for some of his workers. Winter's own house, Winterdyne, was built in the late nineteenth century on the old East Path.

Carnoustie offered residents and visitors alike more sports than just golf. Bowling was also very popular, and one bowling green was situated off Maule Street. This photograph shows a match between the West End Bowling Club and members of Carnoustie Town Council. It appears to have been taken at afternoon teatime, as the gentlemen in the background are enjoying an informal cup of tea.

A group photograph of the town council bowls team and their rivals after the match with the West End Bowling Club.

The Carnoustie Scout Pipe Band of 1927 proudly stands to attention for a photograph. Carnoustie had a burgh band which regularly gave concerts in the town at the Links bandstand and other venues, and also played host to visiting bands.

This group of men and women are believed to be the staff of Kinloch Public School. Fee-paying schools and church schools were prevalent in all Scottish towns until the introduction of the 1872 Education Act which made provision for the setting up of public schools and school boards to run them. For many years Kinloch Public School was the only school in the town, offering elementary education only. Those children who wished to go onto secondary education had to travel to by train to Arbroath or Dundee.

The staff of the World War I Carnoustie Red Cross Auxiliary Hospital in Park Avenue. The nurse in charge was Miss K. Sutherland, seated immediately to the right of Dr Gorrie of the Royal Army Medical Corps in this picture. The man in the background is Sergeant Gray, also of the RAMC. Miss Sutherland, her nursing staff and volunteers looked after hundreds of wounded soldiers from the front lines, and Carnoustie's was reputedly the most popular hospital amongst wounded soldiers in Scotland. It received its first batch of eight wounded men in spring of 1915. During 1918 a second Red Cross hospital operated in Carlogie House under the care of its matron, Miss Kidney.

A large procession marching through Carnoustie, possibly photographed outside the old Co-operative Society shop. It includes members of the town council led by the provost and bailies. The occasion is unknown, but it was traditional for such processions to mark the Kirkin' of the Council, Coronations or the funeral or memorial service of an important local or national figure.

This postcard was sent in 1911 and may have been written by one of the men of the cavalry regiment pictured here grooming their horses at Barry camp. The camps at Barry and Buddon had been used since the 1860s to give the Angus militias better training. The Secretary of War at the time of the Crimean War was an Angus landowner, Fox Maule, Baron Panmure and later Earl of Dalhousie. Between the onset of the Boer War and the outbreak of World War II all of Scotland's Territorial Army and reservists trained at Barry.

Barry Camp. (The Parade)

Artillery at Buddon Camp

During World War I there was a huge influx of soldiers into the camp at Barry, and many regiments including the 10th Seaforths spent time training there. The building on the right was the Soldiers' Home, which provided facilities for off-duty recreation and refreshments. This was extended during World War I to cope with the increased numbers training in the camp. The soldier who sent this postcard to his mother in 1916 described Barry as 'outlandish' because he could not obtain his daily newspaper there!

Buddon camp was used by both artillery and cavalry regiments.

Many Carnoustie men enlisted during World War I; these three were members of the Cameron Highlanders. On 6 November 1925 the *Guide and Gazette* reported on the unveiling of Carnoustie's war memorial, dedicated to the 142 local men who had died in the Great War. The first Carnoustie war casualty was Lance Sergeant Alfred Gooch of the Cameronians, killed in action on 26 October 1914. A row of cottages had been removed to make way for the war memorial which was to be situated in a rest garden, the gift of former Provost George Winter. The money to pay for the work was raised by private subscription, after which the memorial was handed over to the care of the town council. About 3,000 people attended the unveiling ceremony.

Charles Jarvis was the first man to win the Victoria Cross in World War I. He was born in Fraserburgh but spent his early years in Carnoustie. On the outbreak of war, Charles joined up and was sent to France with the Royal Engineers. As Lance Corporal Jarvis he was awarded the Victoria Cross for his actions in blowing up the bridge at Jemappes and thereby helping cover the retreat of the outnumbered British Expeditionary Force from Mons in late August 1914. Jarvis and a colleague set the charges under the bridge from a boat while under fire from Germans. Carnoustie had a second Victoria Cross hero, George Samson. Both men are commemorated in street names, marked by a bronze plaque donated by the British Legion.

Carnoustie has two close neighbours in the fishing villages of East Haven and West Haven. East Haven is a very old fishing village, dating back to the thirteenth century, and during Carnoustie's heyday as a holiday resort was a popular destination for strollers and charabanc trips. In the early nineteenth century the local fishermen supported three boats, giving employment to about eighteen men, and in 1833 the village inhabitants numbered 118. At one time East Haven supported an inn and a brewery, but the village began to decline after 1848 when it was struck by severe scarlet fever, followed by cholera in 1849. Its population levels never recovered. The old houses were considered to be dilapidated and unsanitary and around 1900 all but one of the existing thatched buildings were demolished and new cottages built to a different plan. Electricity and mains water were not introduced until the 1950s.

The charming village of West Haven, which provided a safe haven for mooring fishing boats, has now become part of the burgh Carnoustie.

West Haven from the Beach. Carnoustie

West Haven once attracted its own visitors who enjoyed the quieter beach and the rock pools which appeared when the tide was out. The earliest mention of West Haven and its associated fishings dates from 1507, long before Carnoustie existed as a town. It was always larger, more prosperous and healthier than its neighbour, East Haven. During the eighteenth century it supported a small number of fishing boats and provided a safe mooring for two sloops trading in coal. In 1838 the village was cut in two by the new railway between Dundee and Arbroath, although this offered opportunities for the fishermen to sell their catch in Dundee. The fisher population peaked in the 1880s and then went into decline, following a national trend. By about 1892 West Haven had become part of the burgh of Carnoustie.

C 1348 West Haven, Carnoustie.

West Haven consisted of three main streets – Long Row, East Row and West Row – with a number of smaller rows to the south and west. Its quaint cottages and seaside location made it popular with visitors, especially at weekends.

FEEDING THE DUCKS,
CRAIGMILL,
CARNOUSTIE

A little beyond West Haven there is a path along the banks of the Craigmill Burn through the Den. Craigmill (whose water wheel is visible on the right of this picture) once harnessed the power of the burn for the benefit of the bleach works downstream. It fell into disuse in the late nineteenth century when chemical bleaching made it redundant.

A view of West Haven showing an Arbroath-registered boat pulled up on the shore. Even larger boats such as the coal sloops which regularly brought cargoes into West Haven tended to be beached on the shore like this. Vessels would be steered through the channel, beached on a high tide and relaunched on another high tide. The soldier who sent this postcard to his mother pointed out that the village was larger than it appeared from the picture and that it was more correctly a burgh of barony, rather than a village.

Westhaven, Carnoustie